Family Life Illustrated

for FINANCES

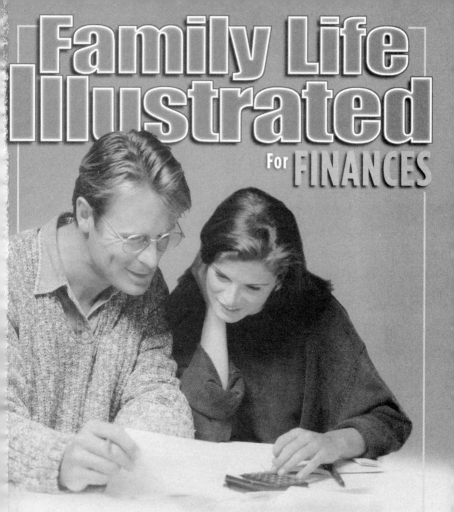

RONNIE FLOYD

Family Life Illustrated

For FINANCES

RONNIE FLOYD

New Leaf Press

Family Life Illustrated for Finances

First printing: November 2004

Copyright © 2004 by Ronnie W. Floyd. All rights
reserved. No part of this book may be used or reproduced
in any manner whatsoever without written permission
of the publisher, except in the case of brief quotations in
articles and reviews. For information write: New Leaf Press,
Inc., P.O. Box 726, Green Forest, AR 72638.

ISBN: 0-89221-587-9
Library of Congress Number: 2004106959

Cover concept by Left Coast Design, Portland, OR

All sidebar statistics have been provided by: The Barna Group
Online, 1957 Eastman Ave Ste B, Ventura, CA 93003.
(www.barna.org/FlexPage.aspx?Page=Topic&TopicID=29)

Printed in the United States of America

Please visit our website for other great titles:
www.newleafpress.net

For information regarding author interviews,
please contact the publicity department
at (870) 438-5288.

CONTENTS

Enormous Challenges

THE financial challenges facing marriages and families today are absolutely enormous. Nothing puts more pressure on you personally and on your family than financial stresses. In fact, nothing will put your marriage more at risk than financial pressure.

A 1997 PBS television special called "Affluenza" reported that arguments about money played a prominent role in *90 percent* of American divorces. A few years later, the producers of that show wrote a book called *Affluenza: The All-Consuming Epidemic*, in which they gave readers a few startling facts to ponder, among them:

- We spend more on shoes, jewelry and

watches ($80 billion) than on higher education ($65 billion).

- Eighty-eight percent of teenage American girls rate shopping as their favorite activity.

- Sixty percent of families have only enough financial reserves to sustain their lifestyles for about a month, should they lose their jobs.

- The average American household carried $7,564 in credit card debt during the year 2000.

- The average size of new homes is now more than double what it was in the 1950s, while families are smaller.[1]

Do you realize that in 2002, over one million Americans declared financial bankruptcy? If a family can somehow avoid a financial trap, they seem to be able to make it through most other challenges in life. In fact, Damon Carr, the owner of ACE Financial, in an article titled

"Until 'Debt' Do Us Part," wrote:

. . . people are more willing to reconcile their difference during the sick times, such as alcohol abuse, drug abuse, diabetes, heart failure, cancer, strokes, and other ailments. People are more willing to reconcile their difference during the worse times like lying, cheating, stealing, verbal/physical abuse, and others. But when it comes to the poor times, nearly 80 percent say it is time to call it quits . . . being financially bound robs you of your security blanket. How can one feel secure when it is a struggle to maintain adequate food, clothing, shelter, and other necessities? Most people do not understand how they got into the financial predicament, let alone how to get out. Being insecure about the necessities of life, not being able to enjoy simple pleasures, and

> If your goal is to have a happy marriage and a healthy family, then you absolutely must come to grips with how you and your family use money.

not knowing how to get out of debt will create a heightened level of stress. The high degree of stress associated with being financially bound is the core reason why financial problems are the leading cause of divorces.[2]

If your goal is to have a happy marriage and a healthy family, then you absolutely *must* come to grips with how you and your family use money. You have no other choice.

In this little book, we'll look into what God says about money and how he expects us to use it. If we begin to manage our finances based on the divine wisdom of God's Word, we

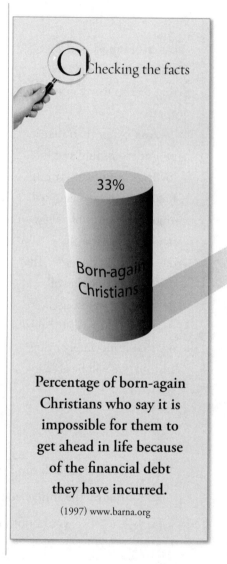

Checking the facts

33%

Born-again Christians

Percentage of born-again Christians who say it is impossible for them to get ahead in life because of the financial debt they have incurred.

(1997) www.barna.org

can avoid most of the terrible pressures and stresses that tear so many homes apart.

And better than that, by understanding and following God's plan for our finances, we can begin to enjoy the Lord's blessings in a way that few these days can even imagine. The disease of affluenza will never infect our households — and neither will the misery that it inevitably brings. Instead, we will be able to say with the Psalmist:

How can I repay the Lord for all his goodness to me?

I will lift up the cup of salvation and call on the name of the Lord (Ps. 116:12–13; NIV).

Endnotes

1 Kristi Turnquist, "Possession Obsession," *Oregonian*, August 26, 2001, p. L9.

2 Damon Carr, "Until 'Debt' Do Us Part," The Dollar Stretcher website, http://www.stretcher.com/stories/03/03nov24f.cfm

> **Measure wealth not by the things you have, but by the things you have for which you would not take money.**
>
> — *From sermonillustrations.com*

If your goal is to have a happy marriage and a healthy family, then you absolutely must come to grips with how you and your family use money. You have no other choice.

Chapter 1

The Facts about Money

"THEY say money talks," goes the bumper sticker, "mine only says good-bye."

For many today, that's the primary fact about money: as soon as they get it, it disappears.

Yet the truth is, the only power that bumper sticker has over us, we give to it. Money does not disappear out of our wallets by magic, and usually not through armed robbery. Much more often, our bank accounts dwindle and our treasuries sag through our own unwise choices — choices that we make without regard to some stubborn biblical facts.

The Book of Ecclesiastes has some powerhouse advice on finances for anyone curious enough to

resources, and fame. The man who had it all looked back over his life and told us like it is.

Fact # 1: Money never satisfies.

"He who loves silver will not be satisfied with silver. Nor he who loves abundance with increase; this is also vanity," writes Solomon (Eccles. 5:10). This king who, in his lifetime, amassed more gold and silver than any ruler then living on earth, tells us that gold and silver can never satisfy. Riches and possessions lack all power to satisfy the soul. Money *never* satisfies.

It reminds me of the often-told story about John D. Rockefeller, one of the richest men of his

look. It was written by a man named Solomon, one of the most powerful and wealthy people who ever lived on earth (1 Kings 3:13; 10:23). The Bible also calls Solomon the wisest man who ever lived (1 Kings 3:12; 4:30–31). At the end of his long life, Solomon bared his soul about the truth concerning money, possessions, generation. Someone asked him, "How much is enough?" He answered, "Just one dollar more." It's just never enough.

As Solomon considered this truth, he pronounced the word "vanity" upon it. The word "vanity" is used 37 times in the Book of Ecclesiastes. Solomon means that money and fame, in and of themselves, produce one only thing: vanity or emptiness. "After I've had

Almost nothing will bring greater pain to a marriage or to a family than financial grief.

it all, done it all, and been with the best of them," he says, "I have to tell you that it leaves you empty. Don't chase money, because money never satisfies."

The New Testament gives a wonderful commentary on this discovery in 1 Timothy 6:9. It says, "But those who desire to be rich fall into temptation and a snare and into many foolish and harmful lusts." And what happens then? What's the end result? Paul says that these foolish and harmful lusts "drown men in destruction and perdition."

So does the fault lie with money itself? Is that the problem? Not according to the apostle, for he goes on to say, "for *the love of money* is the root of all kinds of evil, for which some have strayed from the faith in their greediness, and pierced themselves with many sorrows" (1 Tim. 6:10, emphasis added).

Almost nothing will bring greater pain to a marriage or to a family than financial grief. The Bible says it causes major sorrow. And why would you chase sorrow?

Fact # 2: Money leads to worry.

"The sleep of a laboring man is sweet whether he eats little or much; but the abundance of the rich will not let him sleep" (Eccles. 5:12). Most of us have probably worried at one point or another that we didn't have enough money to meet all our bills. But have you ever considered that men who have more money than they know what to do with spend even *more* time and energy worrying about their riches? Money leads to worry, Scripture tells us. And that worry can grow to such an extent that the owners lose sleep over it.

John D. Rockefeller said, "I have had, or, I have made many millions, but they've brought me no happiness."

W. H. Vanderbilt said it this way: "The care of $200 million is enough to kill anyone. There is no pleasure in it."

Henry Ford said, "I was happier when doing a mechanic's job."

John Jacob Astor, who founded the American Fur

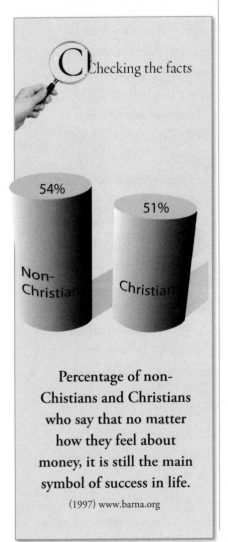

<CHecking the facts>

54%

51%

Non-Christian

Christian

Percentage of non-Chistians and Christians who say that no matter how they feel about money, it is still the main symbol of success in life.

(1997) www.barna.org

Company in New York City, said these words: "I am the most miserable man on earth."

The more money you have, the more you tend to worry about that money. It's just a fact of life.

Fact # 3: Money kept is money lost.

If your goal is making and holding on to piles of money, then listen to what the Scripture says. "There is a severe evil which I have seen under the sun: riches kept for their owner to his hurt. But those riches perish through misfortune; when he begets a son, there is nothing in his hand" (Eccles. 5:13–14).

That is, money kept is money lost.

When someone feels consumed with making and hoarding money, rather than using it to help others, that money has a strong tendency, over time, to sprout wings and fly away. So many of the enormous fortunes of the wealthy industrialists of the past two centuries are completely gone. Why? Because money kept is money lost.

Fact # 4: Money cannot be taken to heaven or to hell.

Regardless of how much money you make and save and hoard, you cannot take even a penny of it with you to heaven or hell. It all stays behind.

"As he came from his mother's womb, naked shall he return, to go as

> *The more money you have, the more you tend to worry about that money.*

he came, and he shall take nothing from his labor which he can carry away in his hand," declares Solomon (Eccles. 5:15). You probably don't remember the way you came to this earth, but you'll go out in the same way: with nothing. You didn't have anything when you came in, and you're not going to have anything when you leave — nothing at all.

So if that's true, why do so many of us live as

though we're taking our money with us into eternity? Why do we live that way? Whether we're on our way to heaven or hell, we're not taking a penny of anything we own with us.

Remember, the more money you have, the more money you will leave behind. Our goal should be to give it all away before we leave this earth, since we cannot take any of it with us.

. . . the Bible insists that pursuing money for money's sake is just like chasing after the wind.

Fact # 5: Money pursued for money's sake is like chasing after the wind.

When we chase after money, when we pursue it for its own sake, the Bible says we are doing nothing more productive than chasing after the wind. What a word for our generation!

And this also is a severe evil. Just exactly as he came, so shall he go. And what profit has he who has labored for the wind? All his days, he shall eat in darkness, and all it does is give him much sorrow, and sickness, and anger (Eccles. 5:16–17).

You can hear the wind, but can you ever grasp it? Can you ever reach out your hand and say, "Look here, I've caught a big gust of wind"? No.

And the Bible insists that pursuing money for money's sake is just like chasing after the wind. It's profoundly unprofitable. And those who insist on it are doing nothing but bringing great judgment on themselves.

Please, don't miss the ugly results of such a life. It's not just that it's unprofitable; it also brings deep loneliness, great sorrow, awful sickness, and terrible anger. And is *that* a life worth living? Do you want to end your life echoing the sad words of John Jacob Astor, who moaned, "I am the most miserable man on earth"?

Fact # 6: God owns everything; you and I own absolutely nothing.

It is not enough to say, as we often do, "God owns everything." All of us feel comfortable with such a statement. But many of us get very uncomfortable when we say, "I own absolutely nothing." Yet the very core fact about money is that God owns it all and you and I own nothing.

Psalm 24:1 tells us, "The earth is the LORD's, and all its fullness; the world and those who dwell in it." The earth doesn't belong to you. It doesn't belong to me. It doesn't belong to big multi-national corporations. It doesn't belong to left wing environmentalists. No! The earth belongs to the Lord. How much of it? All of it. He owns its "fullness."

Look out your window; everything you see there, God owns. Look inside your house; everything you see there, He also owns.

What you and I "own," is in fact, only loaned to us for a little while. And it can be taken away at any time.

God, the Creator, owns it all. He created it, He owns it. When was the last time you created the heavens and the earth? You say you haven't? Then

you don't own it, either. God himself is the absolute owner of everything in existence, which means that you and I own absolutely nothing.

To make sure we get the point, God tells us flatly, "Every beast of the forest is Mine, and the cattle on a thousand hills. I know all the birds of the mountains, and the wild beasts of the field are Mine. If I were hungry, I would not tell you; for the world is Mine, and all its fullness" (Ps. 50:10-12).

To make sure that the ancient Israelites would not forget this truth, God told them when He brought them into the Promised Land, a "land flowing with milk and honey" (Exod. 3:8), "The land shall not be sold permanently, for the land is Mine; for you are strangers and sojourners with Me" (Lev. 25:23).

When was the last time you created the heavens and the earth?

To make sure that the members of the early church did not forget this truth when God blessed them materially, the apostle Paul asked them, "What do you have that you did not receive? Now if you did indeed receive it, why do you boast as if you had not received it?" (1 Cor. 4:7). And he reminded his protégé, Timothy, "We brought nothing into this world, and it is certain we can carry nothing out" (1 Tim. 6:7).

God owns all. That's who He is. God owns everything, and you and I own absolutely nothing.

Fact # 7: Money is a gift from God.

Despite everything we've just seen, don't imagine that the Bible proclaims money a curse.

> "We brought nothing into this world, and it is certain we can carry nothing out"

It never does. What it condemns is the selfish pursuit of money, for its own sake. But take a look at the other side of things.

"Here is what I have seen: it is good and fitting for one to eat and drink and to enjoy the good of all his labor for which he toils under the sun all the days of his life which God gives him; for it is his heritage. As for every man to whom God has given riches and wealth and given him power to eat of it, and to receive his heritage and to receive of his labor — this is the gift of God. For he will not dwell unduly on the days of his life, because God keeps him busy with the joy of his heart" (Eccles. 5:18–20).

Take an inventory of the material blessings you have. What do you have? Whether you have much or little, whether they seem lean or in abundance, they are a heritage from God. They are God's gift to you — not as an eternal possession, but as a gracious loan from heaven. God wants you to use them for His glory and for your blessing. He wants you to use them in the way He has instructed you to use them. And when you do, what is the result? Joy!

When you wisely use the money God gives you, recognizing it for the gift that it is and putting it to the use that God intends for it, the result is a heart *full* of joy! Note the huge

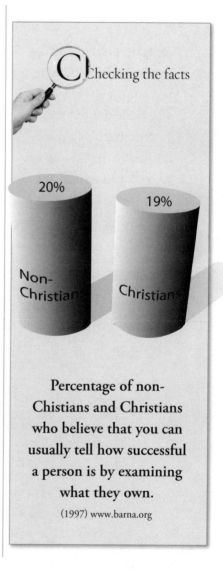

Checking the facts

20% Non-Christians

19% Christians

Percentage of non-Chistians and Christians who believe that you can usually tell how successful a person is by examining what they own.

(1997) www.barna.org

contrast: on one side lies sorrow, loneliness, pain, and emptiness. On the other side there is joy.

Not much of a choice is it, really? Joy or sorrow? Joy or loneliness? Joy or pain? Joy or emptiness?

But which do you choose?

One More Fact

I would like us to consider one more fact about money, but it holds such an important place in Scripture that I think it merits a chapter of its own. In fact, I doubt we should discuss finances and our use of them without considering it.

But I warn you! This last fact about money — if you grasp it and act on it — has the power to totally change your financial life.

Whether you have much or little, whether they seem lean or in abundance, they are a heritage from God.

Chapter 2

A Sobering Evaluation

JOHN Maxwell, a well-known Christian communicator and best-selling author, wrote the foreword to a book titled *The Eternity Portfolio.* In it, Maxwell penned some stirring and challenging words.

"What would happen," he asked, "if we saw giving as a way of investing? If we gave our giving 'portfolio' the same attention we give our retirement portfolio? What would happen if we stopped asking, 'How much do I have to give?' and started asking, 'How much can I invest in eternity by giving?' How would our lives change if we became aware of the rewards of faithfully investing our resources?"

I'm convinced that if we did what Maxwell has

There are two ways in which a Christian may view his money — "How much of my money shall I use for God?" or "How much of God's money shall I use for myself?"

– W. Graham Scroggie

has the power to impact eternity. Eventually I came to understand that heaven operates a rewards system intended to shape and influence the way we give — and the sobering truth is, we will all appear before the judgment seat of Jesus Christ, to give an account of how we have used the resources God has loaned us.

The *Bema* Seat

The apostle Paul makes a sweeping and attention-grabbing statement in 2 Corinthians 5:10. He declares, "For we must all appear before the judgment seat of Christ, that each one may receive the things done in the body, according to what he has done, whether good or bad."

suggested, not only would it change our attitudes about money, it would have the power to change our lives.

Many years ago, during my seminary days, I learned to look at giving as an investment in the future. When later I concentrated my doctoral studies on this theme, I also learned that my giving

Here's the first thing that snares our attention: the apostle doesn't leave anyone out. He says that *every* believer, *every* follower of Jesus Christ, is accountable to Jesus Christ and one day will appear before Him to answer for his or her life. That's a strong statement!

Not one of us who believes, who has a faith relationship with Christ, is

> . . . *heaven operates a rewards system* . . .

left out. All of us, without exception, will stand before the judgment seat of Jesus

Christ. Think of it: one day, your true character will be made known before the searching, penetrating, piercing eyes of Jesus Christ. Most of us spend far too much time worrying about what others might think of us. Has it ever dawned on us that one day we are going to learn what Jesus thinks of us and how we lived our life on this earth?

The "judgment seat" in the Greek language is called the *bema*. In ancient days, two things happened at the *bema*. First, decisions were handed down regarding legal justice. Second, rewards would be given to worthy candidates. Olympic athletes would appear before the *bema*, for example, where winners would receive rewards and crowns for their triumphant performances.

Paul draws upon this image to teach that, one day, every believer in Christ will stand before Jesus to have his or her life evaluated, with rewards handed out to those who have qualified for them.

What kind of things are included in this evaluation? The Bible talks about "the things done while in the body." That covers a lot of ground! Paul has especially in mind your time and your service to Jesus Christ. He is *not* talking about your sins.

Let me try to be clear here. The cross of Jesus Christ takes care of all of your sins — past, present and future. When you, as a believer, stand before Christ at the *bema*, you will never have to answer to Jesus for your sins. Jesus took care of your sins on the cross — done, finished, paid for, completed. You are forgiven.

But one day, you *will* stand before Christ and you *will* answer to Christ for your ministry and for your service to and for Jesus Christ. Paul says you will answer to Him for your deeds, even your financial dealings, "whether good or bad." Good actions in ministry are those that have eternal value. Bad actions are those that have no value in relation to eternity.

So here is the question: do I live my life as if I know I will appear before the judgment seat of Christ? Do I realize that I will give an account for the way I use the resources God has given me?

Do you?

I wonder, did it dawn on you this morning when you got up and began your day, that one day what you do today will be revealed in eternity? Has it dawned on you that if you have an eternal perspective, it should have an impact on your life *even today*? So then, should it not impact your time and how you use your time? If you truly keep in mind that you will appear before the judgment seat of Christ, will it not also impact your relationships and how you conduct those relationships?

And more to the point for this book, will it not also impact your use of the resources that God gives you? Should we not invest all that we have and do in activities that impact eternity?

Many of us who truly know Christ as Savior nevertheless do not live with the recognition that we will stand before Christ to give an account of our activities here on earth. We have allowed ourselves to be lulled to sleep, to think that we're untouchable, that the gentle Jesus would never make us feel uncomfortable in His presence.

May I make it very clear? You and I *will* appear before the judgment seat of Jesus Christ. If you know the Lord, you and your life will be laid bare before Christ. It's not a matter of if; it's a matter of when.

> *. . . we will stand before Christ to give an account of our activities here on earth.*

Three Areas of Evaluation

The Bible tells us not only of the certainty of our appointment with Jesus at the *bema* seat, it also clues us in on the nature of that judgment. Jesus is going to evaluate you and your life in three primary ways.

1. He will evaluate you by what you did.

Jesus will look at your entire life and will evaluate it by what you did. First Corinthians 3:11–15 begins by talking about building your life on the right foundation, Jesus Christ. It then says:

> For no other foundation can anyone lay than that which is laid, which is Jesus Christ. Now if anyone builds on this foundation with gold, silver, precious stones, wood, hay, straw, each one's work will become clear; for the Day will declare it, because it will be

revealed by fire; and the fire will test one's work of what sort it is. If anyone's work is burned, he will suffer loss. But He himself will be saved, yet as through fire.

Remember, this passage discusses the quality of your service to Christ, not whether you have accepted Him as Lord. And it says there are two

ways you can build your life: with gold, silver, or precious stones — which

indicate permanence, beauty, value, and eternity — or with wood, hay, and stubble, indicating things that pass away, that which is temporary, that which is ordinary.

What happens when fire touches wood, hay, and straw? It burns it up. And what does fire do when it hits gold, silver, and precious stones? If it's hot enough, it refines it.

When someone builds his or her life with wood, hay, and straw, they demonstrate that they are living for self, with the temporary in mind, with earthly concerns in mind. Those of us who seriously want to

God will look at your life in regard to all that you did in ministry . . .

prepare for the judgment seat of Christ know that we must build our life upon gold and silver and precious stones — meaning that which will be permanent, that which can pass through the fire of judgment and come out unscathed.

God will look at your life in regard to all that you did in ministry and He will burn up anything that looks like wood, hay, and straw. But He will reward anything that looks like gold, silver, and precious stones. Remember this: only that which you do for Christ, by the power of the Holy Spirit, will last. All else will be useless — wood, hay, stubble — and will get burned up.

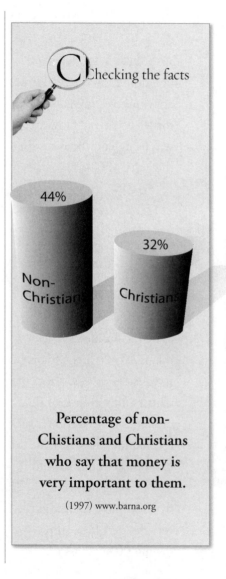

Checking the facts

44%

Non-Christians

32%

Christians

Percentage of non-Chistians and Christians who say that money is very important to them.

(1997) www.barna.org

So may I ask, what are you doing for Christ? How are you investing your life for Jesus Christ? How are you using your finances for the glory of God?

2. He will evaluate you by how you acted as you did.

One day you will stand before God and answer to Him for *how* you did your works of service to Christ. Consider 1 Corinthians 4:1–2: "Let a man so consider us as servants of Christ and stewards of the mysteries of God; moreover it is required in stewards that one be found faithful."

Years ago maritime slaves would languish in the very depths of the ships, rowing them across the sea. Paul has that image in mind in this passage. The word translated "servants" is actually the Greek word that indicates "under-rowers." He means that we are to live for Christ just as those slaves did for their earthly masters. And it doesn't matter how tumultuous the waters become. We must head toward the destination set for us by our Master, making a difference with our lives. We serve Christ as though we're slaves.

Unfortunately, that kind of mentality has largely slipped away from the 21st-century church in America. Most of us want to talk about how good we are, how nobody can do it like us. It's really more about us than it is ever about Him. Sometimes we don't want to play by the rules; we want to create our own rules. May God help us!

We must understand that God will make each one of us answer for *how* we did what we did. And if we stumble at this point in the investigation, we will receive no reward.

Paul says that we are to act as stewards, as managers of a charge entrusted to us. And what is the major requirement of a steward? To be faithful. God wants us to be faithful. He calls us to be faithful.

I wonder, are you being faithful to Christ in your use of finances?

3. He will evaluate you by why you acted as you did.

Christ will also judge you by *why* you did what you did. First Corinthians 4:3–5 says, "But with me, it is a very small thing that I should be judged by you or by a human court. In fact, I do not even judge myself. For I know of nothing against myself, yet I am not justified by this, but He who judges me is the Lord."

God warns us against trying to judge the motivations of another's heart. Very often you don't even know what is in your own

> *How are you using your finances for the glory of God?*

heart, much less somebody else's. That is why Jeremiah says, "The heart is desperately wicked; who can know it?" (Jer. 17:9). And so Paul continues, "Therefore, judge nothing before the time."

What "time" is he talking about? He's referring to the time when the Lord will come to judge His people. That's why we don't have to worry about taking care of everybody

One day Jesus is going to bring all the hidden motivations of our hearts into the light.

else's business and setting everything right. The Lord is going to set it right one day. And how will He do it? The Apostle says He will "both bring to light the hidden things of darkness and He will reveal the counsels of the heart, and then each one's praise will come from God."

The Crucial Question

If you make it through the fiery judgment in relationship to *what* you have done for Christ, *how* you did it for Christ, and *why* you did it, then God says your praise will be from God. God will take care of business and He will bless you in a phenomenal way.

On Judgment Day, Jesus will become a spiritual

cardiologist. He will run tests on you and me far beyond what a cardiologist on this side of heaven can manage. Paul knew that one day he would have to stand before the judgment seat of Christ, and Paul knew that therefore he needed to get his eyes off of people and on Jesus Christ. One day Jesus is going to bring all the hidden motivations of our hearts into the light. Jesus is going to reveal it all.

That thought should either scare you to death or fill you with hope!

So here's the question: do I live my life on earth, knowing that Jesus Christ will evaluate me for *what* I did, *how* I did it, and *why* I did it? Do I use the resources and finances God has given me in such a way that I have everything to gain and nothing to lose at the *bema* seat of Christ?

Wow, what a provocative question! That is the kind of question you need to lay out before the Lord and say, "Now Lord, how can I readjust my life today so that when I appear before Jesus, I can feel optimistic and unashamed in His presence?"

That's really the goal here — spiritual confidence and boldness. The judgment seat of Christ does not have to frighten you.

Even in the way you handle your finances, then, make it your goal to follow the lead of the aged apostle John:

And now, little children, abide in Him, that when He appears, we may have confidence and not be ashamed before Him at His coming (1 John 2:28).

> *The judgment seat of Christ does not have to frighten you.*

The real measure of our wealth
is how much we'd be worth if
we lost all our money.

– *J.H. Jowett*

Chapter 3

Financial Enemies of the Family

A pastor had just finished a sermon on forgiving one's enemies. He asked everyone in the congregation to raise a hand if they now felt willing to forgive those who hurt them. About half raised their hands.

The pastor took a few more moments to clarify the day's teaching, then again asked everyone who was willing to forgive their enemies to raise a hand. About 80 percent of the congregation did so.

The pastor then made several more remarks, and finally repeated his instructions. Everyone in the audience raised a hand — except for Mrs. Jones, the oldest member of the church.

"Mrs. Jones, why aren't

you raising your hand?" the pastor asked.

"I don't have any enemies," she replied.

The surprised pastor invited Mrs. Jones to come to the front and then asked her, "Mrs. Jones, I hope you don't mind my asking, but how old are you?"

"I'm 93," she answered.

"And could you tell us," the pastor asked, "how you could live so long on this earth without having any enemies?"

"It's easy," Mrs. Jones said. "I outlived them all."

It would be nice if we could outlive our financial enemies, but that's just not going to happen. The only way to deal with the potent enemies of our household finances is to identify them, target them, and decisively deal with them. In this chapter I'd like to discuss just a few of the most troublesome of these financial enemies.

1. Ignorance

Many of our households get into financial trouble because we remain ignorant about a number of important issues regarding money and its use. We are ignorant about the purpose of money, ignorant about giving money, ignorant about saving money, ignorant about spending money. And the list goes on and on.

If you do not know what God says about each of the areas just mentioned, then I urge you to do whatever it takes to get yourself informed. Read

> . . . only two out of ten Americans . . . know how to balance a checkbook.

some good books on the topic by a trusted advisor, such as Ron Blue. Educate yourself in what God has

to say about the proper and wise use of money. Don't remain ignorant when you have it in your power to educate yourself!

2. No financial plan

Many of us get ourselves into trouble because we have no financial plan, no accurate record keeping, no thought toward the future. In fact, the vast majority of people I speak with have no financial plan at all.

Recently I read from a reliable source that only two out of ten Americans even know how to balance a checkbook. How tragic!

We live in the day of the ATM. You take out

your little card, put it in the machine, type in your code, and out comes money. Cool! But do you know what is happening to the American family? More and more are suffering from what I call ATM trauma — one day they go to the well too often, and nothing's there. It's empty. And they're dumbfounded. Flat broke! And do you know why? Because they have no financial plan.

3. A wrong attitude

We're bound to get into financial trouble when we begin with the attitude, "It's all my money, and I'll do with it whatever I want." As we've already noted, *none* of it really belongs to us. God owns everything; we own noth-

ing. He graciously loans us the use of various resources, but they're His to recall whenever He so chooses.

Recently I read a sad story about James K. Craig Jr. of Hebron, Indiana. James won $9.7 million in the Indiana state lottery, the Hoosier Lotto. He quit his factory job, took a trip to Cancun, Mexico, and skied in Colorado. But just a few weeks after he won the jackpot, the 43-year-old man died after his car hit a utility pole in a rainstorm. It was the second time in 2004 that an Indiana lottery winner died soon after claiming the jackpot. In January of that year, Carl D. Atwood, 73, was struck and killed by a pickup truck just hours after winning $57,000 on

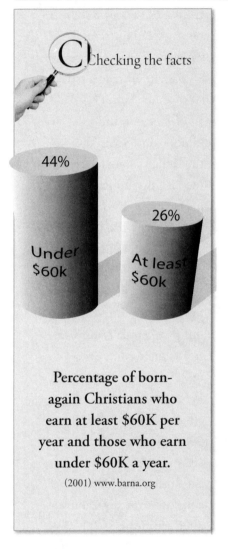

hecking the facts

44%

26%

Under $60k

At least $60k

Percentage of born-again Christians who earn at least $60K per year and those who earn under $60K a year.

(2001) www.barna.org

the "Hoosier Millionaire" television show. He was killed while walking to the store where he had bought the winning ticket.[1]

That reminds me of the parable Jesus told in Luke 12 about a rich man who kept getting richer, and who supposed that all his wealth came to him through his own hard work and shrewdness. When the man's portfolio continued to grow, without any thought of God, he determined to build bigger warehouses to store all his growing stuff. It seemed to make perfect sense — until God said to the man, "Fool! This night your soul will be required of you; then whose will those things be which you have provided?" Jesus then put the capstone on His lesson: "So is he who lays up treasure for himself, and is not rich toward God" (Luke 12:20–21).

It really isn't all your money; it's just on loan to you for a time, from God. In fact, not even your body is your own, if you count yourself a Christian. The Bible tells us explicitly that "You are not your own," and that "you were bought at a price; therefore glorify God in your body and in your spirit, which are God's" (1 Cor. 6:19–20). So if not even your body belongs to you, how much less the resources that God puts at your disposal?

> *It really isn't all your* money; it's just on loan to you for a time, from God.

4. A credit mentality

Our culture has gone wild on using credit. Everywhere you turn, you're urged to use other people's money — at a steep interest rate. Banking institutions and credit companies try to convince you that if you will just use their funds, you will be able to accumulate much more stuff at a quicker rate.

But of course, a day of recompense is coming. You do have to pay back everything that you borrow, and then some!

Did you know that, in the year 2000, the American Credit Counselor's Corporation estimated the average American credit card holder owed *$13,000* to credit card companies? That's right — thirteen thousand dollars!

The National Association of Colleges and Employers reports that 22

> *. . . compared to 1992, credit card debt is up* 173 *percent in this country.*

percent of college students owe more than $7,500 on credit cards.

So what, you ask? Here's so what. If you carry a $7,000 balance on an 18 percent interest credit card — the standard rate — and pay just the 2 percent minimum each month, you'll wind up paying *more than $20,000* for that $7,000 loan. So all those things you bought at half price, that you felt so good about? They're going to cost you *at least three times* what you paid the store for them.

In addition, Citibank calculates that a consumer using a credit card will buy 26 percent more than he would if he were carrying cash, even if he paid it all off at the end of the month without incurring interest charges.

In 2002, credit card debt was up nationally 8.5 percent. Compared to 1997, credit card debt is up 36 percent. And compared to 1992, credit card debt is up *173 percent* in this country.

Don't get sucked into a credit mentality. It will rob you of your future. A credit mentality seriously injures and even destroys the family. It is a major enemy of the family's finances.

5. *Excessive debt*

Excessive debt is a tremendously powerful enemy that all of us need to fight. Stay away from debt as much as possible on depreciating items!

While the Scripture never forbids debt, it does talk a great deal about the importance of repaying your debts. It also issues strong warnings about indebtedness, especially extreme and excessive debt.

The car payment, the house payment, the credit card bills — they come in regularly, every 25 to 30 days, and you are accountable to pay them. Make sure you don't get into a position where you find it impossible to cover all your debts, or where you find yourself "robbing Peter to pay Paul." If you must incur debt, make sure that you have the ability to pay it off. Don't get in so deep that you see the surface of the water from your grave, two miles down.

6. Impulsive spending

Have you ever heard (or participated in) a conversation like the following?

"Honey, I saved $40 today because I got this dress on sale. It was originally $100, but I got it for just $60."

"Did you need a new dress?" he replies. "Did you plan for that dress in your budget?"

> *God's will for His children is not that they get rich quick.*

"No," she says, "but I saved you $40."

But here's the question: Did she really save $40?

No! In reality, she spent an unplanned $60, which means she lost $60 from her budget. Do that too often, and you're headed for disaster.

Several men were sitting around in a locker room at a golf club. A cell phone on a bench rang, a man engaged the "hands-free" speaker function, and began to talk. Everyone else in the room stopped to listen.

"Hello," says the man.

"Honey, it's me," says a woman's voice. "Are you at the club?"

"Yes," he replies.

"I am at the mall now and found this beautiful

leather coat," she says. "It's only $1,000. Is it okay if I buy it?"

"Sure, go ahead, if you like it that much."

"I also stopped by the Mercedes dealership and saw the new 2005 models. I saw the one I really like."

"How much?"

"$60,000."

"Okay," he says, "but for that price, I want it with all the options."

"Great! Oh, and one more thing. The house we wanted last year is back on the market. They're asking $950,000."

"Well, then, go ahead and give them an offer — but just offer $900,000."

"Okay, I'll see you later. I love you!"

"Bye!" says the man, "I love you, too."

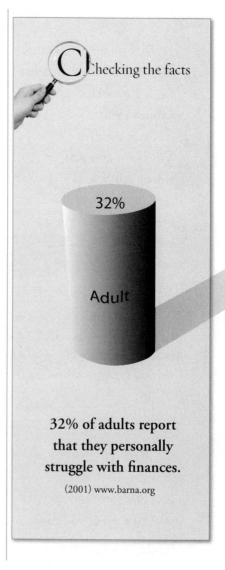

Checking the facts

32%

Adult

32% of adults report that they personally struggle with finances.

(2001) www.barna.org

As the man hangs up, the other men in the locker room are looking at him in astonishment.

Then the man asks, "Anyone know who this phone belongs to?"

Beware of impulsive spending! Make sure you're not that man or that woman!

> *And if we use the funds that God gives us according to His instructions, God will bring no sorrow on them.*

7. Get rich quick schemes

There is no such thing as getting rich quick, so don't let some promoter or salesman get to you emotionally.

Remember the words of Proverbs 21:5: "The plans of the diligent surely lead to advantage. But everyone who is hasty comes surely to poverty."

God's will for His children is *not* that they get rich quick. God's plan for His children is that they work hard, plan carefully, and reap the rewards of what He has enabled them to acquire — not so that they can spend it all on themselves, but so that they can advance His kingdom and help others in need. As the apostle Paul says, "You will be made rich in every way so that you can be generous on every occasion, and through us your generosity will result in thanksgiving to God" (2 Cor. 9:11; NIV).

Our Greatest Financial Ally

While we face difficult challenges from many financial enemies, let us never forget our greatest financial ally. May I remind you of what kind of God we serve? Proverbs 10:22 says, "It is the blessing of the LORD that makes rich, and He adds no sorrow to it."

If you use your finances in a way that honors God and follow His instructions, it doesn't matter what you have or don't have. If you have what God wants you to have, you're a rich man or a rich woman.

The truth is, the lowest paid individuals in this country are wealthier than the vast majority of the rest of the world. And if we use the funds that God gives us according to His instructions, God will bring no sorrow on them. God never brings financial sorrow upon you when you abide by His principles and live according to His book.

And He'll also take great pleasure in keeping those nasty financial enemies of the family at bay.

Endnotes

1 http://www.member.compuserve.com/new/html/live/scoop/cs/7.html

Chapter 4

A Six-Step Formula for Financial Health

THERE are all kinds of formulas in life. They surround us, even from birth.

We begin life by tasting various baby formulas — some, more tasty than others.

In junior high and high school, we begin to learn various math formulas — some, more daunting than others.

In college, we study some high-powered scientific formulas — some, like Einstein's $E=mc^2$, that blow our minds.

In the work world, some of us have to learn various industrial formulas — some, more profitable than others.

But in this chapter, I'd like to suggest another kind of formula, a simple one

Book? Are you handling your finances by taking into account God's view of money? That's the place to start.

This Bible is the Word of God, accurate in every way. And because it's perfect and represents the perfect God who gave it to us, it is to serve as our authority on all economic issues. While it is not a financial book, it does speak to finances, and when it does so, it declares exactly what is right in God's eyes. And if you willingly follow its wisdom, He will bless you for it.

Your ultimate financial authority is not Wall Street. Your ultimate authority is not your accountant. Your ultimate authority is not your checkbook.

you can use to help bring your family into financial health. If you carefully follow the six steps to this formula outlined below, you stand an excellent chance of avoiding the financial catastrophes that swallow up other families.

1. Live by a biblical view of money.

Are you living by the

A Six-Step Formula for
Financial Health

If you are a Christian, your ultimate authority must be the Word of the Lord.

Living by a Christian world view means that you understand the Bible's take on money and its place. Did you know that the Savior of the world, Jesus Christ, spent at least 15 percent of His recorded words in Scripture speaking about money and posses-

> *Your ultimate financial authority is not Wall Street.*

sions? Now, why would He do that? He did so because He knew that a powerful relationship exists between our true spiritual condition and our attitude and actions toward money and possessions. Consider just one of the Master's pointed teachings on money:

> Do not lay up for yourselves treasures on earth, where moth and rust destroy and where thieves break in and steal; but lay up for yourselves treasures in heaven, where neither moth nor rust destroys and where thieves do not break in and steal. For where your treasure is, there your heart

will be also (Matt. 6:19–21).

If someone were to observe your life for a month, where would they say your heart lies? Would they pinpoint its location to treasures on earth, or in heaven?

2. Give God, through His church, at least 1/10th of all God has given to you, immediately after receiving it.

If you want to posture your family toward financial health, then give back to God, through His church, at least 1/10th of all God has given to you, immediately after receiving it. This is one of the greatest things you can do for the financial health and prosperity of your family.

In Scripture, this is known as the "tithe." A tithe is simply 1/10th of all that you earn or receive. That includes your salary, your bonuses, your bonds, your stocks, your property. Malachi 3:10 says, " 'Bring all the tithes into the storehouse, That there may be food in My house. And try Me now in this,' Says the LORD of hosts, 'If I will not open for you the windows of heaven And pour out for you such a blessing That there will not be room enough to receive it.' "

I believe that you endanger your family's financial future until you begin to live by this biblical practice. How can the Lord bless disobedience? So whatever income or assets you receive, immediately

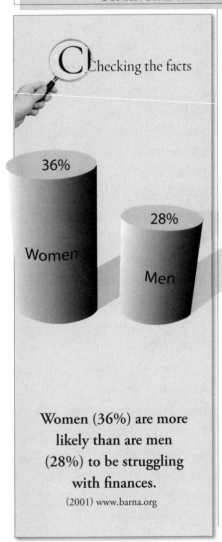

Checking the facts

36%

28%

Women

Men

Women (36%) are more likely than are men (28%) to be struggling with finances.

(2001) www.barna.org

give to the Lord at least ten percent of it. And it doesn't matter how rich or poor you are.

Perhaps you say, "I can't afford to do that!" Listen, you can't afford *not* to do it! The greatest insurance policy you have regarding your family's financial future is to operate by this biblical principle. And the greatest mistake you can make is to ignore it or reject it.

Perhaps you say, "Well, I've done pretty well without it." But the end has not yet come, friend. Remember, one day you will stand before the judgment seat of Jesus Christ. And if you reject His Word now, what will He say to you then?

Acts 4:32–37, one of the most dynamic passages in the Bible, illustrates how the early disciples viewed the privilege of giving. Verses 34 and 35 say, "All who were possessors of lands or houses sold them, and brought the proceeds of the things that were sold, and laid them at the apostles' feet; and they distributed to each as anyone had need." That's powerful! Can you imagine it?

The early disciples modeled for us the *unselfish* nature of giving that ought to characterize every believer in Christ. And how could they be so unselfish? They knew that nothing belonged to them; God owned it all. So it didn't seem so hard to use the resources God had given them to help out their needy brothers and sisters in Christ.

How can the Lord bless disobedience?

Second, these believers encouraged and adopted a *sacrificial* attitude. They were willing, even eager, to give away "their" stuff for the advancement of the kingdom of God. This sacrificial attitude dominates the text as much as anything else.

Of course, in a more accurate sense, the word "sacrifice" doesn't really work, since these believers clearly believed that no one actually "sacrifices" anything when they give something to God for His use. God will be a debtor to no one. Probably they remembered Jesus' words: "Assuredly, I say to you, there is no one who has left house or brothers or sisters or father or mother or wife or children or lands, for My sake and the gospel's, who shall not receive a hundredfold now in this time — houses and brothers and sisters and mothers and children and lands, with persecutions — and

in the age to come, eternal life" (Mark 10:29–30). We may call the giving of the early church "sacrificial," but in the final analysis, it was only a good investment.

We find a third crucial attitude of biblical giving in 2 Corinthians 9:7–8. There the apostle Paul writes:

> So let each one of us give as he purposes in his heart, not grudgingly or of necessity; for God loves a cheerful giver. And God is able to make all grace abound toward you, that you, always having all sufficiency in all

God loves a cheerful giver.

things, may have an abundance for every good work.

Paul tells us that God loves a *cheerful* giver. The word translated "cheerful" means upbeat, positive, enthusiastic about giving, as opposed to reluctant givers who show a dour or resentful attitude about their gifts. To Paul, giving to the Lord's work had much more to do with privilege than duty. He never got over the fact that God had tapped him on the shoulder and invited him to serve heaven's interests, even through his giving. He counted it an incredible blessing.

Do we?

We need to pray, "God, make me unselfish. God, help me to be cheerful in my giving. And Lord, I pray that You will help me to understand that any 'sacrifice' I make will be repaid many times over, in this life and in the one to come."

If anyone ought to understand the power and the blessing of giving, it ought to be God's people. You're never more like God than when you give.

3. Avoid the credit and debt trap.

If you have a credit card and don't make it a habit to pay the full balance at the end of each month, then you need to perform immediate plastic surgery in your purse or your billfold. Cut up those cards and so break their hold over you.

If you don't or can't pay off your credit card balances in full each month, then they will destroy you financially. Get rid of them!

You may be a young adult, a college student, even a high school student. It doesn't matter. Don't let the extravagant interest rates of credit cards strangle your family finances. Nothing will destroy your finances more quickly than the unwise use of credit cards. And if you must go into debt, be wise about it, and try your best to go into debt only over appreciating items.

4. Live within your financial means.

Refuse to listen to those silly ads that insist you "deserve" this or that item or vacation or car or house, even if you can't really afford it. Reject the "buy now, pay later" mentality. If mail order catalogs prompt you to buy things you can't afford, then get rid of the catalogs. Write to the companies that send you their catalogs and tell them to stop sending you their materials. Do whatever you need to do to start living within your means.

If you are a Christian who has decided to live by God's principles, then you do not have to reach for a lifestyle that demands 125 percent of your actual income, or even 90 percent of it, for that matter. Consider the example of John Wesley, the great evangelist and church planter of three centuries past.

Wesley consciously limited his expenses so that he would have more to give to the Lord's work. In 1731, Wesley's income amounted to 30 English pounds and his living expenses to 28 pounds, so he had two pounds to give away. The next year his income doubled, but he still managed to live on 28 pounds, so he had 32 pounds to give away. In the third year his income ballooned to 90 pounds, but instead of allowing his income to dictate his spending and lifestyle, he lived on 28 pounds and gave away 62 pounds. The next year, his income rose to 120 pounds, but — you saw this coming, didn't you? — he

> *Reject the "buy now, pay later" mentality.*

continued to live on 28 pounds, and gave away 92 pounds. Wesley continued this practice throughout his life. One year, in fact, his income rose to 1,400 pounds; he lived on 30 and gave away the rest. Even when his income rose to thousands of pounds, he chose to live simply and gave away his surplus.

Learn to live within your means! And then train yourself to be generous.

5. Remind yourself that all you have is a gift from God.

Land, property, house, money, stocks, bonds, inheritance — whatever it is — it all comes as a gift from God. So live as though every bit of it is a gift that God has given you. And be grateful.

It doesn't matter how much you have or don't

> *. . . many among us try to get our worth from what we own.*

have. Everything you have is a gift to you from God. Remember, God owns everything and you and I own absolutely nothing. I know such a bold statement makes a lot of people uncomfortable. It intimidates them. It frightens them. Why? Because many among us try to get our worth from what we own. Don't you be one of them! If you are living like that, then you are skating on thin ice and are only moments from an uncomfortable (and unnecessary) fall into the icy waters below.

6. Make a plan.

Sometimes, clichés are just that — catchy little sayings that either state the obvious or declare what hardly needs to be said in the first place. You know the kind:

*In two shakes of a
lamb's tail*

Crazy as a bed bug

*To pay through the
nose*

*That's how the cow
eats the cabbage*

Sometimes, you hardly
know what a cliché even
means. But at other times,

the cliché "hits the nail
on the head," so to speak.
I think one of the best in
that category is the following maxim:

> *Those who fail to
> plan, plan to fail*

It may be a cliché, but it
still rings true. Sometimes,
"pat" answers are dead on.
And it's certainly true in
this case. When it comes to
family finances, the failure

to craft and apply a plan invites failure and welcomes disaster.

I have some great news for you. You do not have to fret over finding the right financial plan. You do not have to give up all of your magazines and all of your Christian literature in order to determine the right plan for your life.

I want to challenge you to embrace wholeheartedly *God's* plan as revealed in the Bible. For thousands of years, God's plan has been tested, tried, and proven. This plan will not only impact your life today, but will impact your life for all of eternity.

You do not need to reinvent God's plan, nor do you need to try to reengineer it. While it does not need to be modified, it does need to be codified — that is, it needs to become your code of behavior. And once you do make it your code of behavior, God will be able to do some things in your life far beyond your imagination. And by the way, it's guaranteed by God himself.

What more do you need?

Many of us have heard God's plan for salvation and have embraced it without any reservation. Many of us are aware of God's plan for marriage and family, and a vast majority of us have embraced it. But when we come to this financial plan of God, many of us seem to want to redefine it, ignore it, deny it, or try to just act as if there is another way. But there is no other way.

The Bible gives us God's financial plan in 1 Chronicles 29:3, where David says, "Moreover, because I have set my affection on the house of my God, I have given to the house of my God over and above all that I have prepared for the holy house, my own special treasure of gold and silver." I consider this verse a microcosm of God's plan for securing your family's finances.

Prior to this, David had assembled the leaders of Jerusalem to tell them that he had it in his heart to build the temple of God. But because David was a man of war, God would

> *. . . the failure to craft and apply a plan invites failure and welcomes disaster.*

not let David build the temple. God had a better idea. The Lord chose David's son, Solomon, to build the temple. Solomon may have been as young as 20 years old when he began this construction project.

David gave Solomon plans for the temple which he had received from the Holy Spirit as recorded in 1 Chronicles 28:12. David donated gold and other substantial resources from his own estate to build it.

A Six-Step Formula for Financial Health

David assured Solomon that "God will be with you," and then David told him that willing craftsmen would also assist him. In fact, all of the leaders and all of the people would support him as he did God's work.

So David made extensive preparations to help his young son build the temple of God, and he did so "with all my might"

> . . . you will give yourself in giving, if you've already willingly given yourself to God.

(1 Chron. 29:2). David also encouraged the people and their leaders to give themselves to this great task: "Who then is willing to consecrate himself this day to the LORD?" (1 Chron. 29:5). His question reveals an important biblical principle: you will give yourself in giving, if you've already willingly given yourself to God. And that is exactly what the people did.

The people gave additional billions of dollars worth of materials to the project. And the Bible says, "Then the people rejoiced, for they had offered willingly, because with a loyal heart they had offered willingly to the LORD; and King David also rejoiced greatly" (1 Chron. 29:9).

That is always the pattern; once you give yourself to God, all other kinds of giving start to flow naturally and joyfully. That's why we see the same thing in the New Testament. In 2 Corinthians 8:5, the apostle Paul says of some financially poor converts who still wanted to give materially to their suffering brothers in Jerusalem, "And not only as we had hoped, but they first gave themselves to the Lord and then to us by the will of God."

When David saw what was happening in his own time, he could not help but open his mouth in praise to God. He praised God for His bounty: "For all that is in heaven and in earth is Yours" (1 Chron. 29:11). He praised God for His grace in the life of the king and his people: "But who am I, and who are my people, that we should be able to offer so willingly as this?" (1 Chron. 29:14). And he praised God for the ability to give: "For all things come from You, and of Your own we have given You" (1 Chron. 29:14).

In other words, it's our blessing to do God's work.

David then says, "I know also, my God, that You test the heart and have pleasure in uprightness. As for me, in the uprightness of my heart I have willingly offered all these things; and now with joy I have seen Your people, who are present here to offer willingly to You" (1 Chron. 29:17).

God tests our hearts through giving! Did you know that? David's people passed the test. How? Because they first offered themselves willingly to God. And when someone does that, it paves the way for all his or her financial bills to be taken care of.

I believe that's the heart of God's plan for healthy family finances.

The Formula Works

It's a simple formula, even if I don't know how to write it with fancy mathematical symbols:

Live by a biblical view of money + give God His tithe + avoid the credit and debt trap + live within your financial means + remind yourself that all you have is a gift from God + make a plan = financial stability.

I may not be much good at math, but I know this formula *works* — so long as you put it into practice. And when you do, you're well on your way to the kind of financial health that millions of Americans can only dream about.

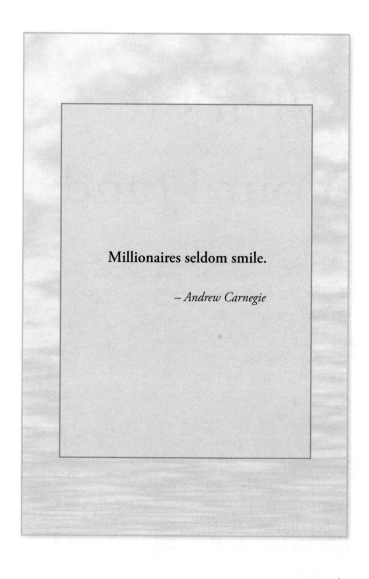

Millionaires seldom smile.

– *Andrew Carnegie*

Chapter 5

What's in Your Hand?

FINANCIAL health does not depend on having a lot. It does not depend on earning a huge salary. More than anything else, it depends on listening to what God says about your use of money, and then allowing Him full use of whatever He puts in your hand.

I can hardly think of a better illustration for this crucial point than Moses.

Times of Preparation

For the first 40 years of his life, Moses lived as a prince in the house of Pharaoh. He learned all the wisdom of the Egyptians and enjoyed all the perks of royalty. He probably thought he was being prepared for a distinguished career in the service of

Pharaoh. God was preparing him, all right, but for something completely different. God was preparing him for something great, something powerful, and something most unusual.

Eventually, Moses began to learn that he was not, in fact, an Egyptian, but rather a Hebrew. One day he saw an Egyptian overseer abusing a Hebrew slave, and in a fit of rage, Moses killed the abusive man. His rash action cost him everything he had achieved to that point. For the next 40 years, Moses was forced to live on the back side of the desert, all because he had acted rashly and in anger.

The story of Moses highlights the providence and power of God. While Moses languished in the desert during those second 40 years of his life, God spoke to him. One day God showed up in a desert bush that kept burning, yet was not consumed. God called Moses that day to return to Egypt to free the people of God, the Hebrews, from the tyranny and oppression of the mighty Egyptian empire.

It was not an assignment that Moses accepted gladly! More on this a little later.

Moses debated with God. He tried to persuade God that He'd be better off with someone else at the helm. But God knew what He was doing, and Moses eventually accepted the divine assignment.

So in the third segment of Moses' life, after his

then helped those same people move toward the land of promise. The Book of Exodus chronicles all of these amazing events.

Assess Your Assets

As we just saw, Moses did not accept God's assignment eagerly. In fact, he did everything he could think of to talk God out of the job. Listen in to just part of Moses' argument:

> . . . *Moses did not accept God's assignment eagerly.*

80th birthday, Moses returned to Egypt to lead his kinsmen to freedom. Moses

Then Moses answered and said, "But suppose they will not believe me or listen to my voice? Suppose they say, 'The LORD has not appeared to you?' "

So the Lord said to him, "What is that in your hand?" He said, "A rod." And He said, "Cast it on the ground." So he cast it on the ground and it became a serpent, and Moses fled from it. And then the Lord said to Moses, "Reach out your hand and take it by the tail" (and he reached out his hand and caught it and it became a rod in his hand) "that they may believe that the Lord, God of their fathers, the God of Abraham, the God of Isaac, and the God of Jacob, has appeared to you" (Exod. 4:1–5).

Prior to this exchange, Moses had already tried to sabotage his job interview. He asked God, "Who am I, that I should go back to Egypt to do this?" (Exod. 3:11). When that didn't work, he tried a second excuse: "If they say to me, 'Who sent you?' who do I tell them?' " (Exod. 3:13). God told him, "I will be with you, Moses, and you tell them that. And you also tell them that the great I AM is sending you back. When you return to Egypt, Moses, you will have authority — and I will be with you."

And now Moses, sensing his list of excuses growing thin, asks God, "What if they do not believe me or listen to what I say? What will I tell them?"

Somewhere in the middle of this debate between Moses and God, the lights began to get turned on. Moses started to see that his life was about to change in a radical way for the better — different from anything he had ever known, but better. Do you know what God said to him? "Moses," He said in essence, "assess your assets." That's what the Lord meant when he asked Moses, "What is that in your hand?"

Did you know that, what God asked Moses, He's also asking you? "What is that in your hand? Take a look at your assets. What is in your hand?"

God was telling Moses, "List your assets. What do you bring to the table, Moses?"

Moses replied, "Well God, I've got a rod. That's all. An old rod, nothing more."

A rod was a staff, something like a walking stick. As Moses walked through the desert, he needed assistance. He needed something to help him to remain stable while trekking through the rough terrain, so he found himself a sturdy walking stick. Some suggest it was like a shepherd's crook. But whatever the rod may have been, Moses used it for several things. He used it to steady himself over rugged land. He used it for protection. He used it for punishment and discipline among the flocks he cared for. He also used it for measurement.

> *Take a look at your assets. What is in your hand?"*

Still, it was only a stick. And Almighty God, for some reason, took an interest in it.

"What is in your hand, Moses?" the Lord asked. "Assess your assets, Moses. You're arguing with me about where I want you to go and about what I want you to do. I'm telling you, you have to start with where you are and with what you have. Now, what do you have, Moses?"

"I have a rod."

God was trying to get Moses to invest all that he had into his work. Perhaps you say, "Well, he sure didn't have much." On one level, you're right. He didn't. But on another, Moses had great treasure.

In fact, God had two great things there. He had a rod, and He had Moses.

That's all God needs! Really, God doesn't even need a rod, if He has you. But if He has you — truly *has* you — then He has all of you, including everything you are, everything you have, everything you think you own, everything in your future.

May I ask the same question of you that God asked of Moses? What is that in your hand? What are you holding onto? What do you bring to the table to contribute to the expansion of the kingdom of God around the world? What do you hold in your hand that God may want to use? What do you hold in your hand?

Think about the resources you have: house, car, stocks, mutual funds, retirement accounts, insurance policies, quarterly dividends on investments, salaries, performance bonuses, recreational equipment, timeshares, jewelry, equity from the sale of a home or sale of property, rental

Moses stammered when he spoke and had nothing but an old stick.

property, antiques, or collectibles. What do you have in your hand?

Most of us bring far more to the table than Moses did. Moses stammered when he spoke and had nothing but an old stick. Nevertheless, God turned Moses into a great prophet of the Lord. How? The first step occurred when God challenged him to assess his assets.

Once you understand what you bring to the table, God will tell you the same thing He told Moses. And what was that?

"Throw it down."

Moses didn't have much, but what he had, God told him to release. God told him to throw it down. God instructed Moses to throw down the rod — all that he had in his possession. And in obedience to God, Moses threw it down.

And guess what happened next? When Moses threw down the rod, it became a snake. So Moses did what any Spirit-filled Christian would do: he ran! Before he ran, though, Moses obeyed God.

Will you obey God? Will you throw down what is in your hand? God directed Moses to give up all he had, even though all he had was a rod. And do you know what God said to him?

"Give it to Me."

Perhaps you're saying, "I don't have a lot." It doesn't matter. God doesn't need a lot. Centuries after Moses' time, a

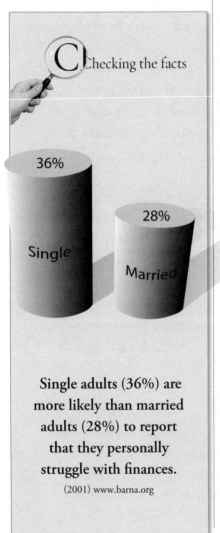

Checking the facts

36%
Single

28%
Married

Single adults (36%) are more likely than married adults (28%) to report that they personally struggle with finances.

(2001) www.barna.org

destitute Israelite widow came to Elisha the prophet with a terrible problem. Her creditors were threatening to take away her two sons and sell them into slavery in order to pay her household debts. What could Elisha do for her?

"Tell me," Elisha said to her, "what do you have in the house?"

"Your maidservant has nothing in the house but a jar of oil," she replied.

What did she have? She looked around and replied, "Nothing." So Elisha instructed her to borrow as many empty jars as she could and to start filling them with the little oil she had in her own jar. She kept filling and filling, and somehow her "nothing" got transformed into abundance. She sold the "miracle oil" (think how much she could have earned had she known about advertising!) and with the proceeds paid off her creditor — and still had some left over to live on (2 Kings 4:1–7).

God doesn't need much. Even "nothing" will do.

Perhaps you say, "I'm not much." Then you're in good company. Both the patriarch Abraham and the apostle Paul said of themselves, "I am nothing" (Gen. 18:27; 2 Cor.12:11).

Nevertheless, God wants every part of all you are and all you have. "Throw it down," God says to us. "Give it to Me. Transfer ownership back to where it belongs."

Are you willing to throw them down? Are

> *God doesn't need much. Even "nothing" will do.*

you willing to obey Christ? Throw them down!

I know this for sure: you'll have a hard time throwing down your assets if you're not first willing to throw down the greatest asset you have — you. Are you willing to throw yourself down and to throw down all that God has entrusted to you?

"And why should I do that?" you ask. You should

do so because of a third thing God did in Moses' life, the same thing God wants to do in your life. God wants to use you and your assets in a miraculous way.

As we said, God doesn't need a lot. But if He ever gets anything, He can turn it into a whole lot more. When Moses threw down his rod and God turned it into a snake, Moses ran. I think he probably broke

> *We worry that we'll lose if we do things God's way.*

the 100-yard dash record. And then do you know what God told him?

"Moses, turn around and get back here."

Despite his fear, Moses obeyed. He walked back toward God. And God said, "Moses, you see that serpent? You see that snake?"

"Yes, Lord."

"I want you to reach down and pick it up."

"Pick it up, Lord? You want me to pick up the snake?"

"Yes, I want you to pick it up."

Just as Moses took a big breath and was about to lean down to pick up the thing, God said to him, "Moses, I want you to pick it up by the tail."

Moses had to stumble on that one!

"Pick it up by the tail, Lord? But if I pick it up by the tail, that leaves the busy end open!"

And God said, "Moses, you do it My way."

Late one October, Jeana and I were walking on a vacant lot, with me leading the way. When I walk, I tend to walk straight ahead, looking in the direction I'm moving. When Jeana walks, on the other hand, she tends to looks down.

Jeana saw something before I did. It was long and black and within one foot of my foot. She didn't say anything at first, but when she realized it was a snake, she hollered, "Ronnie, watch that snake!"

Immediately I got filled with the Holy Ghost. I started jumping with joy and danced all around that lot. That thing scared the living daylights out of me! I cannot stand snakes. In my opinion, the only good snake is a dead snake. But since I had nothing on to use to kill that snake, I began to pick up some pebbles and rocks. Soon that snake began to coil up toward me. Even today, it makes me shudder to I think of it.

As quickly as I could, I tossed my rocks and hit the snake in the back. And I thought, *Surely, that will get it.* Believe me, I didn't want that snake or his brothers or cousins any-where around me!

If God would have told me that day, "Ronnie, you

pick up that snake — and do it by the tail," I think I would have joined Moses in his 100-yard dash. I doubt I would have had his faith to pick up that snake by the tail.

But that's exactly what Moses did. He reached down by faith, picked up that serpent by the tail, and as soon as he had done so, it turned back into a rod.

What great faith Moses had! But in fact, he also had his best interests at heart. Once he felt convinced that God wanted to do great things through him, he willingly cooperated.

The only assets Moses had, his life and the rod, God asked him to throw down. And only after he threw them down, did God say to him, "Now, Moses,

you can pick them back up."

I think it's exactly here where so many of us struggle. We worry that we'll lose if we do things God's way. But God says to us, "You will never, *ever* lose if you do things My way."

In fact, we lose only one thing when we decide to do things God's way: control. And I know that bothers a whole lot of us. If we would only remember that life isn't about us, but about Christ, I think it would bother us a whole lot less.

Back to Moses. Finally, he was ready for his new assignment. The Bible tells us, "Then Moses took his wife and his sons and set

them on a donkey, and he returned to the land of Egypt. And Moses took the

> *If we would only remember that life isn't about us, but about Christ . . .*

rod of God in his hand" (Exod. 4:20).

Did you see what just happened there? Or did you miss it? Before this incident in the desert, Moses had only a rod. Although his rod became a serpent, it was still just a rod. But now, it's different. Something has changed. It's not what it used to be. The rod of Moses is no longer just a rod; now it's "the rod *of God.*"

This tells me that it doesn't matter what you

have in your hand. It doesn't matter how important or insignificant you think you are. When you throw it down and when God gives you permission to pick it back up, it won't be yours anymore; it will be God's. And then you'll no longer be operating merely in the natural. Then you'll be operating in the supernatural from that time forward.

> *. . . what do you have in your hand? What does God want you to throw down?*

From that day on, you'll be able to watch the hand of God at work in your life. You'll be able to watch the amazing things that God chooses to do with your assets. And remember, God specializes in taking that which is very natural, and doing something extraordinary and supernatural with it.

And as if that weren't enough, it doesn't end there!

Look what happened next in the life of Moses. God said to him, "When you go back to Egypt, see that you do all those wonders before Pharaoh *which I have put in your hand*" (Exod. 4:21, emphasis added). Amazing! God put the power of God in Moses' hand!

God took the old rod of Moses and turned it into the rod of God, which became a symbol of God's power. With it Moses did supernatural wonders.

That is what God wants from you. *That* is what God wants from me. *That* is what God wants from every teenager, every college student, every mom and dad, every single adult, every senior adult, every widow. That is what God wants from *you*.

All God wants is you and that which is in your hand. And He will take it and turn it into something far greater than anything you can imagine.

When you hold on tightly to what you think you have, you limit what God will do with you. So why would you want to hold on to it? Throw it down!

Do it God's way. It only makes sense, because God takes little and turns it into much. God takes much and He turns it into more.

So let me ask once more: what do you have in your hand? What does God want you to throw down?

Start with your life. Don't worry about the stuff until you're willing to start with you. When God called me to the ministry in 1972, He didn't say, "Now, you bring all of your stuff." I didn't have any stuff; I had me, that was all. And that's all God wants. Singer Ethel Waters was right when she used to say, "God plus you equals a majority."

And then throw down your assets. You have all kinds of assets, far beyond what you might think. Throw them down. Give them to God. If you do, you'll watch God turn them into moments of power, into tools of greatness.

Why limit your life or your finances when all God needs is a little, which He'll turn into much? And then He'll take your much and turn it into more.

So throw it down. You always win big when you go with God, and when you do it God's way.

. . . God specializes in taking that which is very natural, and doing something extraordinary and supernatural with it.

Jesus Christ said more about money than about any other single thing because, when it comes to a man's real nature, money is of first importance. Money is an exact index to a man's true character. All through Scripture there is an intimate correlation between the development of a man's character and how he handles his money.

– Richard C. Halverson

PHOTO CREDITS

Corbis: 27

Getty: 41

Money and Finances: 13, 63

Photos.com: 7, 20, 37, 53, 71

Seniors: 74, 82

SuperStock: 11

Also by Dr. Ronnie Floyd . . .

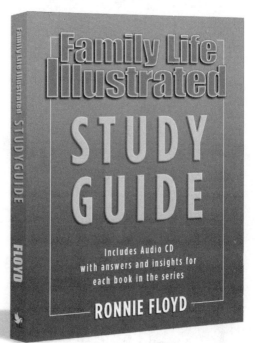

ISBN 0-89221-599-2

Special Features Include:

• Study questions in each book for reflection and to aid
  small-group study

• Study guide that works for all six books that also includes
  an audio CD from Dr. Floyd with answers and insights for
  each book.

5 1/4 x 8 3/8 • Paper • 128 pages
• *INCLUDES AUDIO CD*

Available at Christian bookstores nationwide.

Also by Dr. Ronnie Floyd . . .

ISBN 0-89221-583-6

Are you happening to life or is life simply happening to you? Overwhelmed, overworked, stressed, and tired, it's easy to lose sight of things important to you as a woman, wife, and perhaps even a mother. Be empowered, be decisive, and be open to God's gently guiding hand in your life! God can be what you need – He can strengthen, calm, and sustain you when life seems impossible. No matter what you face, God can give you the knowledge and wisdom to adapt, endure, and affect a change!

Available at Christian bookstores nationwide.

Also by Dr. Ronnie Floyd . . .

ISBN 0-89221-586-0

It seems like everything keeps changing and no one understands. Every day seems to bring more pivotal decisions to be made. Life is complicated and stressful, and you feel you are alone! Fight the isolation – don't be a spectator in your own life! Get powerful solutions and strategies to survive and thrive during the toughest time of your life – and find out how to rely on God when life overwhelms you!

Also by Dr. Ronnie Floyd . . .

ISBN 0-89221-588-7

Your job, your finances, your friends – nothing you ever do will matter as much as being a good parent to your child. Going beyond the surface strategies and quick psychobabble solutions, this book reveals solid, God-based insight on becoming a more effective parent. Don't choose to struggle alone — tap into the wealth of wisdom God wants to share with you and find how you can make a positive, remarkable, and lasting change in the lives of your children today!

Available at Christian bookstores nationwide.

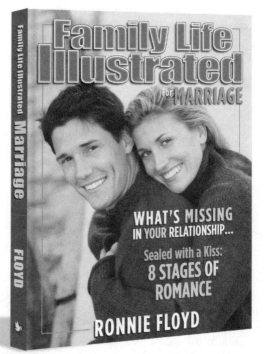

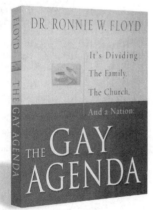

About the Author . . .

Recognizing the vital importance of the family in the success of not only individuals, but for our society today, the "Family Life Illustrated" series offers real answers for real-life problems being faced each day by families. Articulate, informative, and always relevant — Dr. Ronnie Floyd is reaching the hearts of millions weekly through his broadcast ministry Invitation to Life, aired on WGN's Superstation and other television networks nationally each week. An accomplished author of 17 books as well as a powerful group speaker, Dr. Floyd has over 27 years of ministry experience and is senior pastor for a congregation of 15,000 in Northwest Arkansas. Dr. Floyd has been been seen on Fox News, WorldNetDaily, Janet Parshall's America, Washington Watch, USA Radio Network, FamilyNet, and more!

MORE RESOURCES FROM
DR. RONNIE W. FLOYD

CD/VHS/DVD
"Family Life Illustrated Series"

CD/VHS/DVD
"The Gay Agenda"

Other Books By Dr. Floyd
Life on Fire
How to Pray
The Power of Prayer and Fasting
The Meaning of a Man

Weekly International Television and Internet

Sundays: (7:30 a.m. CST) WGN SUPERSTATION

Thursdays: (9:00 p.m. CST) Daystar Christian Television Network

Sundays: (9:15 a.m. CST) Live webcast on
www.fbcspringdale.org

For more information on all resources: www.invitationtolife.org

For information about our church:
www.fbcspringdale.org   www.churchph.com

or call (479) 751-4523 and ask for Invitation to Life